QUEEN ROSHAUNDA ALEXANDER

THE LITTLE GIRL WHO WANTED A CAT

WORKBOOK PRESS LLC
187 E Warm Springs Rd,
Suite B285 Las Vegas NV 89119 USA

Website: https://workbookpress.com/
Hotline: 1-888-818-4856
Email: admin@workbookpress.com

Ordering Information:
Quantity sales. Special discounts are available on quantity purchases by corporations, associations, and others. For details, contact the publisher at the address above.

ISBN-13: 978-1-958176-74-0 - Paperback Version

PUB. DATE: 10/16/2025

QUEEN ROSHAUNDA ALEXANDER

THE LITTLE GIRL
WHO WANTED A CAT

DEDICATION PAGE

This is a way of acknowledging those who have helped me along the way.

My deepest appreciation to….

All those who encouraged me and helped me in prayer, project, and financial support to bring this book to completion to my family and to Ameerah Naajidah Bilil. My beautiful daughter who enjoys playing with her cat named, " SECRET".

I want to thank also my friends and relatives; this book would not be complete without you.

Most importantly, my gratitude to the Lord and Savior Jesus for His grace and companionship during this project and the Holy Spirit's faithful guidance through this assignment.

Once upon a time, there was a little girl named, "Star" who always wanted a cat. Everyday she would ask her mommy when are you going to get a cat for our house? And her mother would say out loud, A cat in this house? And the girl would say, "yes mommy, a cat in this house".

So one day, the mother woke the little girl up out of her sleep. The little girl yarned, "yes Mommy, why are you waking me up so early on a Saturday morning?" The mother said I have a surprise for you. Let's take a walk down the street.

After getting dressed and eating a good breakfast, the girl named STAR said, "mommy, look at those cats in front of that lady's house".

Her mom said, STAR let's count out loud how many cats we see? One, two, three, four, five, six, seven, eight, nine and ten so star and her mommy counted ten beautiful fluffy cats. The black cat with green eyes was STAR's favorite cat to watch.

As Star and her mother walked back home, there was a gray cat sitting on their front porch as if it was saying Please feed me. I have NO place to live. STAR said out loud, "Mommy, Mommy please! Can we keep this cat?

Her Mommy said, STAR let's just go back in the house and pray about it, then tomorrow at 8:00 PM, I will let you know if you can keep a cat in our house.

EDITOR'S COLLECTIVE

THE LITERARY REPORTER

Championing Stories, Celebrating Voices.

Milestone Reached! Your Feature Page for Mother Daughter Bond engaged 98 readers this past month!

Dear Roshaunda,

Great news! Your feature page for Mother Daughter Bond has captured the attention of 98 readers this past month. Your growing audience is a testament to your craft, and we couldn't be more delighted for you.

Click here to view: https://theliteraryreporter.com/book-submission/mother-daughter-bond/

Should you have any inquiries, please do not hesitate to reach out.

Here's to an even wider readership discovering Mother Daughter Bond in the coming months!

Your friends from the reading nook,

The Literary Reporter Editorial Curation Team

Biography & Memoir

"Every writer needs two selves—the generative self and the editor self"
Mary Karr

Art in the Crossfire

By Stephen Freeman

Careful, old Letters

By Alexandra Davidson

Reflections to a Paper Moon Book from the Pages

By L A Cyprus

Mother Daughter Bond

By Rashaunda Alexander

Reflections to a Paper Moon Book One Golden Glow

By L A Cyprus

Secrets Are Out Now: How a Girl Over The World

By Crystal Rivers

Mother Daughter Bond

By Rashaunda Alexander